Beauty of
Ohio

Beauty of
Ohio

Text: Robin Will
Concept & Design: Robert D. Shangle

Second Printing August, 1992
Published by LTA Publishing Company
Division of Renaissance Publishing Company, Inc.
318 East 7th St., Auburn, IN 46706

"Learn about America in a beautiful way."

Library of Congress Cataloging-in-Publication Data
Will, Robin
  Beauty of Ohio / text, Robin Will.
      p.   cm.
    ISBN 0-914343-83-1: $19.95. — ISBN 0-914343-82-3 (pbk.): $9.95
    1. Ohio — Description and travel — 1981 — Views.
2. Ohio — Description and travel — 1981 — Guide-books.
I. Title.
F492.W68   1989
917.7104'43 — dc20   89-38293
CIP

Contents

Introduction

When white men came into the area that now is Ohio, they found, quite simply, the largest deciduous hardwood forest in the world. Under the trees was land that could double or triple the yield of the thin New England soil, and under the land, though no one knew it at first, were other riches: oil, natural gas, coal, iron ore. It was the sort of place where success seemed assured; all that was needed was someone to do the work.

They were not long in coming. When Ohio joined the Union in 1803, 196 years had passed since the first permanent settlement on American shores. The eastern seaboard was crowded, society stratified, and opportunity in short supply. Settlers started trickling into Ohio, struggling through the Appalachians and moving down the Ohio River in flatboats. Where they landed they made clearings and planted crops, opening the dark forests, and getting sunlight to the fertile ground for the first time.

The new land seemed to engender a new attitude; even very early observers made note of the buoyant optimism that permeated Ohio, the yeasty mix of people and resources that made things happen fast. Perhaps it was the fresh start where, lacking a common past, people invested together in the future. Certainly the natural richness of the land encouraged optimism and accomplishment. It was a place in those early years, at least, where a man's abilities were his only limitations, and where hard work *would* pay off. The earth offered of itself in ways the settlers had never dreamed of, and progress seemed inevitable.

Ohio found out soon enough that there's such a thing as too much "progress", and, being Ohio, it came up with something else. Call it progressivism, the ability of a people to evaluate what they're doing, to build on accomplishments, to master "progress", and make it work for them. Agriculture is an example. Progress produced so much wheat in the new frontier that it was burnt for fuel or used to fill mudholes. So, progressive people built canals to get the crop to market. When it became apparent that the world would buy all the grain Ohio could produce, progressive farmers developed machines like the nation's first mechanical reaper to help them keep up with the demand. And when their lands started to wear out from overuse, progressive Ohio farmers began research on land conservation and crop diversification. Every move has been a gaining move.

Agriculture was not the only area where "progressivism" sharpened, improved, and diversified the first fruits of success. Runaway industrialization produced exploitation and corruption, while, at the same time, progressivism produced the nation's first unemployment compensation program and the author of the Sherman Anti-Trust Act. Progress produced environmental pollution, overgrazing, over-logging, and runaway erosion; and educated Ohioans, seeing what they had wrought, developed the nation's first nature conservancy.

Ohioans know that in spite of the soap, pottery, matches, Bibles, rubber products, playing cards, golf balls, pumps, power shovels, cash registers, and coffins, in whose production they lead the world, everything still comes back to the land. Farming is still the largest single industry in Ohio, and occupies nearly 70 percent of the land. Outside of the major metropolitan areas, and Ohio has seven, the Ohio countryside continues to offer up its riches. The list of Ohio's agricultural products reads like a menu: livestock, poultry and eggs, wheat, sugar beets, maple syrup, rye, vegetables, orchard fruits, a half-million gallons of wine a year, and, for the after-dinner smoke, tobacco. Industrial Ohio attracts most of the attention, but the traveler who gets outside of town will find a country that still treasures and depends on the good land that was there in the first place.

The white man changed Ohio's face more than anything since the Ice Age. Only fleeting glimpses remain of the great hardwood forest. It was cleared, stump by painful stump, so Ohioans could grow food, get it to market, fuel the steel mills, pump the oil, make the glass, and supply industry with its raw materials. The land has been used, and in some cases, it has almost been used up.

However, man's influence on the land has not been all bad, and Ohio, early to reap the consequences of irresponsibility, has made haste to improve its stewardship. As a result a traveler in Ohio will see rich and well-managed croplands, groves of sugar-maples, lush pastures, while lands that never should have been plowed are being reforested. Then there are the lakes. To start with Ohio had about 6,700 acres of natural lakes, while, today, about 100,000 acres are under water. Reservoirs were built to feed the canals, and later ones impounded water for navigation or for relief from the disastrous flooding that has plagued Ohio for all its history. The lakes attract migratory waterfowl, wildlife, and people.

Mindful of their ties to the land and their need for natural beauty, Ohioans have been far from backwards in reserving for public use the beautiful, the primitive, and the unusual. Parks dot the Lake Erie shoreline, and Hocking Valley, underlain by sandstone that was once the shoreline of an earlier lake, shows in its fascinating erosional patterns just what a river can do when it is hurried along by a glacier.

In other places Ohio has memorialized its history, the remnants of the Ohio and Erie canal in Miami County, and its prehistory in the Indian burial mounds that dot the state. Even the conservation movement, itself, has been honored. Ohio Power Company Recreation Area in northeastern Morgan County is a rehabilitated strip mine where clear-running streams and narrow, winding valley lakes have brought even the beaver back to land once mined for coal to produce electricity. And Malabar Farm, once the home and laboratory of conservationist farmer and writer Louis Bromfield, is now a state park and a monument to the conservation movement.

Typically for Ohio, preserving the land has turned out to be good business. Ohio was not the first state to awaken from 19th-century capitalism to find itself polluted, eroded and overgrazed, but it *was* the first state to develop a nature conservancy district. The $40-million expense of the first project has already had direct benefits of more than $90 million, and Ohio's example has served as a model for federal legislation. Another success story is in the making as Ohio cleans up, re-forests, and regenerates, an example of energy, education, and ingenuity making a real contribution to the progress that has always been part of the Ohio character.

Ohio will never again be covered by the world's greatest deciduous hardwood forest. That distinction is gone with the Indians who once walked the forest trails and camped in the great subterranean caves. This land, once a playground for the massive forces of ice-age glaciers, is now gently rolling farmland, reshaped by man. But because of man, as much as in spite of him, Ohio is still beautiful, more beautiful, perhaps, because it is more appreciated by those people, who in a day of industrialization, still know the value of their land.

The problem with a book like this is selection. How can a small book deal with such a big subject? The four dozen photographs we present can only suggest the beauty of the free and wild spaces of Ohio, the orderly farms, the mighty rivers, the canyons, lakes, and waterfalls. We can no more than hint at what's there, perhaps enough to whet the appetite and flatter the pride of those Ohioans and others who want to know what lies outside of the seven metropolitan areas that get most of the attention. We offer this book as an appetizer. The reader is responsible for discovering the main course, the State of Ohio, on his own.

— Robin Will

Miami, Adena

The Ohio River runs from the coal hills to the corn belt, defining the south border of the State of Ohio. Early settlers struggled through the Appalachians to Pittsburgh, bought flatboats, and floated down the Ohio until they found some likely place to put ashore. In the absence of other highways, the "shining road" of the Ohio River, broken only once along its length by rapids, provided a main means of transportation into a new frontier. Centuries later, it is still an important shipping artery, though no longer the only one.

If you were to put a flatboat into the river at Pittsburgh now, to duplicate the journey made in the 1780s and 90s by Ohio's settlers, the first half of the journey would be made through fairly industrialized and developed country. The shipping of iron ore and coal, and the production of steel and ceramic products, keeps the river bustling with traffic and the banks developed to receive and discharge the freight that flows up and down the river.

Below Portsmouth, however, the landscape changes to a serene, pastoral setting. In some areas fields and forest roll down almost to the water's edge, smaller creeks and rivers intersect, and it's possible, discounting a few locks and dams, to get an idea of how things looked in an earlier time. The peaceful river flows at about three-miles-per-hour, regulated now by dams and canals to provide the constant nine-foot depth needed for year-round navigation. Where the river bends gracefully to disappear between wooded hills, and the *Delta Queen* makes a stately appearance through the sunlit haze, then just for an instant the river offers its immutable experience: time might be suspended, and you may mur-

mur, ". . . so *this* is how it was." It seems to be the nature of rivers everywhere to allow people, occasionally, to become unstuck in time, and the Ohio will show you where it has been if you're patient.

The river was there before the settlers came, and so were the Indian mounds that dot southwestern Ohio. It is another kind of experience in timelessness to ponder the massive earthworks of these peoples who have been forgotten by history. Tremper Mound, outside of Portsmouth several Ross County sites around Chillicothe, and three sites on US Highway 50 and Ohio Highway 41 between Chillicothe and West Union, have been set aside as memorials to these people. In other places the plow, road construction, and archaeological probing have unearthed bones, tools, and weapons of the vanished mound builders, and it has been possible to recognize these distinct cultures from the artifacts they left behind.

Earliest and most advanced of the mound builders were the Hopewell tribe, and since the mounds are actually graves, most of what is known relates to how the Hopewells disposed of their dead, or at least some of their dead. Along with cremated remains, pottery, pipes, woven fabrics, ornaments of copper, mica, and pearl were placed inside the burial mounds. Awls and needles of bone, and terra cotta figurines have also been found. The Hopewell people placed earthworks around their burial mounds, and beneath some of the mounds were elaborate systems of interconnecting pits and tunnels. At the Seip Mound between Bainbridge and Chillicothe, exposed archaeological diggings show the outlines of ceremonial workshops.

Later, but more primitive, cultures such as Adena and Fort Ancient sometimes overlap the Hopewell remains. Fort Ancient, which was a Hopewell ceremonial site some 2,000 years ago, was later occupied by the Fort Ancient culture, which is characterized by crude pottery, ornaments of stone, bone, and shell, and generally uncremated human remains. Today a nature trail offers picturesque views of the Miami River valley on the way to the three "forts" at the Fort Ancient site. The Adena culture, more advanced than Fort Ancient but less so than the Hopewells

12

who preceded them, were responsible for the great conical mounds, containing single or multiple burials as well as copper, fabric, and beaded artifacts.

The largest, most spectacular, and most famous of the prehistoric Indian earthworks is the Serpent Mound, located on State Highway 73 between Loudon and Locust Grove. The mound is in the shape of a wriggling snake with an egg in its jaws. Built by the Adena Indians for some inscrutable ceremonial purpose, the mound unwinds for 1,300 feet across a gentle hilltop through a grove of trees. An observation platform allows you to take in the whole scene at once, providing a chance to soak up the mystery and significance of this strange place in the green and rolling hills.

A few other locations near the Ohio River give you a chance to think back — way back. North of Chillicothe, the Mound City Group National Monument, a large geometric complex is known as the "City of the Dead." Twenty-three mounds surrounded by an earth enclosure served some ceremonial function at about the time of Christ. And in northern Jackson county near the village of Leo, northwest of Jackson on US Highway 35, is the Leo Petroglyph. A large rock outcrop provided an opportunity for some ancient prehistoric artist or artists, probably Fort Ancient Indians. Many objects are recognizable: birds, fish, a mammal that is most likely a bear, human feet, and animal tracks. The messages, if in fact they are messages and not just prehistoric doodlings, have so far escaped translation.

History along this part of the Ohio stretches back clear out of sight: before the white man there were Indians, and before those Indians there were *other* Indians — and before that, there were glaciers. Southwestern Ohio owes much of the variety of its landscape to the effects of the tons of ice that once ended there: even the lands that were not scoured by the massive icecaps were eroded by the runoff when they melted, and some streams, blocked by ice and rubble, were forced to relocate through higher ground. The result is, generally, rolling landscape, punctuated in places by deep gorges cut through bedrock as the glacial melt added power to the displaced streams.

Some of the resulting gorges are spectacular enough to preserve as state parks, although many remain private property. Caesar Creek, Seven Caves, and Rocky Fork are samples that belong to the public; Caesar Creek and Rocky Fork are on artifical lakes of the same names, and Seven Caves is only a short distance from Rocky Fork.

Caesar Creek is a few miles east of Waynesville, on State Highway 73. The deep valley of Caesar Creek gorge was carved out by great quantities of glacial meltwater. The canyon walls rise a breathtaking 180 feet above the valley floor, and the exposed limestone is rich in fossils.

Similar forces created Rocky Fork's valley. The gentle topography is due to glacial smoothing and deposits that filled the original stream valley. In the lower valley below the dam that impounds Rocky Fork Lake, it is possible to see the gorge cut when Rocky Fork was crowded by the Wisconsonian glacier.

At the intersection of Paint Creek and Rocky Fork is Seven Caves State Park, likewise created by the erosive power of glacial meltwater. Trails have been developed to give hikers access to the caves. This area, with deep, rugged gorges, winding streams with waterfalls, and lush vegetation on rocks and in the valleys, inspires a sense of wonder. The caves are rich in Shawnee Indian lore.

Farther north and west, right up against the Indiana state line, is another area worth visiting for a feel of the "original" Ohio: Hueston Woods State Park, outside of College Corner. Though surrounded by products of human engineering, Hueston Woods presents a 200-acre forest of virtually uncut beech and maple, a remnant of the big woods that once covered three-quarters of the state. Some of these magnificent hardwoods exceed seven feet in diameter, and the first branches are as much as 70 feet above the ground. Aside from the trees there's a dammed stream creating a 625-acre lake for swimming, fishing, and boating.

Plenty of history has happened in southwestern Ohio since the coming of the white man, as well. Miami University in Oxford was the home of William McGuffey, author of the *McGuffey Readers*, which brought literacy to whole generations of Americans. His home, on the Miami University campus where he taught between 1826-36, has been preserved with period furnishings. Another location that allegedly resulted in a book is the Rankin House in Ripley, the restored home of an agent in the Underground Railway. Visitors can climb the stairs, which were used by slaves who were escaping to freedom, and enjoy a spectacular view of the Ohio River from the house. It is said that here Harriet Beecher Stowe heard the story of Eliza crossing the ice, an episode which she wrote into *Uncle Tom's Cabin*.

Of course, southwestern Ohio is canal country, and Miami and Erie Canal Park, between Hamilton and Middletown, preserves recreation areas, forest tracts, and some restored sections of the canal. A hiking trail along the old towpath adjoins the Rentschler Forest preserve, an oak, gum, maple, and hickory forest with steep limestone ravines. The canals were virtually abandoned long before the turn of the century, and most were seriously damaged by the disastrous flooding in 1913. Natural succession is turning them back into woodlands.

In Lawrence County north of Ironton is the Dean State Forest, established in 1916 as the second forest acquired for timber management and wildlife protection. The forest lands on this property were cut over for charcoal to fire the iron furnaces that operated in Ohio before 1830, until richer sources of iron were discovered in Michigan and Minnesota. This is typical Allegheny plateau country, with deep, rugged gorges cut by creeks that erode the sandstones, limestone, and coal with which the area is underlain. A forest hiker can get a good look at the accomplishments of progressive timber management and an intimate view of some impressive hickory woods.

The Vinton Furnace Experimental Forest outside of Dundas occupies 1,200 acres of land that was clear-cut more than 100 years ago to make charcoal for the Ohio blast furnaces. The land now has timber approaching 100 years of age, and since 1952 the Mead Corporation, in cooperation with the U.S. Forest Service, has been conducting research here on soil types and species selection for reforestation in the varied topography of southern Ohio. Field trips or tours must be scheduled through the Mead Corporation in Chillicothe, but nothing will keep you from driving past for a look, $3^1/_2$ miles east of Dundas, off State Highway 93.

Marblehead Lighthouse

Upper Falls, Old Man's Cave Area, Hocking Hills State Park

North of Hillsboro

Mohican State Park

Stan Hywet Hall and Gardens, Akron

Old Man's Cave Area, Hocking Hills State Park

Sandusky River, Crawford County

Ash Cave, near Logan

Shawnee Lookout Park

Waterfall near Yellow Springs

Sunset at Fort Meigs, Perrysburg

Cincinnati

Hocking Hills State Park

Kelly's Island

Paint Creek Lake

Cleveland

Cincinnati

Lyon's Falls, Mohican State Park

Covered Bridge, Washington County

Lantern Court, Kirtland

Soybean Farm near Toledo

Early morning in Ohio Farm Country

Park of Roses, Columbus

Holden Arboretum, Kirtland

Cleveland City Greenhouse

Hopkins Old Water Mill, Garretsville

September Afternoon in Rural Ohio

Krohn Conservatory, Cincinnati

Crosby Gardens, Toledo

President McKinley Memorial, Canton

Cincinnati Nature Center

Sharon Woods, Sharonville

East Harbor, Marblehead Peninsula

Piqua Historic Area

Downtown Columbus

Covered Bridge near Mansfield

Farmland near Buckeye Lake

Hocking Hills State Park

Farming near Berlin

President Harding Memorial, Marion

Covered Bridge near Yellow Springs

Rock Creek Canyon near Kankakee

Indian Mill, Wyandot County

The Ohio River, near North Bend

Near Windsor

Millersburg area farming

Mill Creek Park, Youngstown

Near Fitchville

Lake Plains
and Tecumseh

The west was one of the last regions settled and developed in the rush for land in Ohio. However, the area filled up rapidly after a few minor problems were solved, and the attributes of the area became known.

While settlers were drifting down the Ohio River on flatboats in the 1780s, the area at the tip of Lake Erie was occupied by Indians who were becoming resentful of the white man's incursions. Toledo, at the mouth of the Maumee River, enjoyed some settlement after General Wayne won the Battle of Fallen Timbers in 1794, but the little lakeside settlement was abandoned during the War of 1812.

However, a good seaport, even one surrounded by swamps, cannot be kept down, and the city of Toledo, Ohio, was chartered in 1837, after several years of wrangling with Michigan over possession.

The glacier-smoothed lands south and west of Toledo, heavily forested and poorly drained, proved fertile and productive when cleared, and the area got all the boost it needed when the Wabash and Erie Canal from Lafayette, Indiana, went through to Toledo and was opened in 1843. Two years later, the Miami and Erie Canal was cut through some of Ohio's highest country to join the Wabash and Erie at Defiance, and the rolling plain country of northwestern Ohio came into its own.

Early maps of Ohio identified this area simply as "Black Swamp," an area about the size of Connecticut stretching from Toledo south to Findlay, and west nearly to Bryan. The area was all dense forest of the type that doesn't mind getting its feet wet: elm, ash, cottonwood, and sycamore, punctuating miles of bog and swampland. It was devoid of settlement until the mid-nineteenth century. Canal building in the Maumee Valley drained some of it, and the first settlers in the area were the middle Europeans who had been brought in for canal labor. When work ended on the Miami and Erie, they kept right on moving into the swamp, opening the rich black earth to sunlight for the first time. Today all that remains of Black Swamp is the name, but over near Defiance, adjoining AuGlaize Village on the windswept plain, is Black Swamp Farm, which is operated in the 19th-century style.

The original Black Swamp was a relic of one of the prehistoric predecessors of Lake Erie, and south and west of Toledo is another interesting place that was the sandy shore of a prehistoric glacial lake. The area is called Oak Openings, a throw-back to the time when natural clearings were so rare that it made more sense to name the clearing than the forest around it. Though the lakeshore is now far away, Ohio's only living sand dunes are right here at Oak Openings on this ancient beach ridge, nourishing a variety of oak species and incredible numbers of plant and animal life found nowhere else in the region.

A great deal that's worth seeing in the northern part of this region has to do with the canal construction in the 1800s. In 1932 the Toledo Metropolitan Park District signed an agreement with the State of Ohio to operate the abandoned Miami and Erie Canal lands in Lucas County as a park. Several hundred acres are set aside along the Maumee River, connecting Providence, Bend View, and Farnsworth Parks. Some of the nicest views of the peaceful Maumee River are to be found here, and at Side Cut Park you can see the original limestone locks through which canal boats first entered the Maumee River in 1843. At Providence Park a picturesque dam on the Maumee, built to feed water into the canal, is the main attraction. The park, itself, is located in what was the old town of Providence, a thriving town until an epidemic of cholera closed it down. Canals got the agricultural economy of the country booming, but in less than a generation, the output of the rich farmlands became too great for canals and towboats, and railroads captured the imagination of the public. The canals declined steadily, and many segments were destroyed by the heavy flooding of 1913.

The biggest boom in the northwest, literally, was in Hancock County, on the southern edge of the Black Swamp, when the Karg gas well exploded. Long before the commercial discovery of oil, itinerant preachers were warning Hancock County farmers that the fires of hell were burning directly below them, and farmers frequently had to deal with the nuisance of striking gas rather than water when they sank a well. A few actually piped the stuff into their homes for heat and light.

It wasn't until the middle of the 1880s that any serious efforts were made to utilize the natural gas. In 1886, after 24 days of drilling, the Karg well exploded with a "boom" heard across the country and a plume of fire 100-feet tall. Before they got the well under control, the glare was visible for 40 miles, and for a half-mile around, grass grew green within a circle of snow, and crickets chirped all night. Findlay's gas ran low by 1890, but few people minded because oil had been discovered as well. Findlay is still home base for Marathon Oil Company.

Zane Caverns, a similar formation, are a few miles away, outside the town of Bellefontaine. The caverns are relatively small, but the aboveground scenery is quite varied. After exploring the caves it's possible to hike through an old oak-hickory forest at one of the highest points in Ohio.

Farther south is the city of Dayton, which deserves mention here because of the Miami Conservancy District, one of the nation's pioneering flood-control projects. Though Indians had warned earlier settlers about flooding, the attractiveness of the Miami River's direct trade route to Cincinnati over-ruled other considerations, and the city of Dayton grew at the intersection of three rivers and a creek: the Miami, the Stillwater from the north, Mad River from the east, and Wolf Creek from the west. There were floods in 1805 and 1814, but the citizens built levees and crossed their fingers. A flood control project was actually planned, contracts were let, and construction equipment in place when the skies darkened on March 23, 1913, and rain commenced to fall. By the time the rains stopped, three days later, Dayton was drowned.

Even while the town was still mopping up, money was subscribed for a flood control program and the state legislature passed the Conservancy Act of Ohio. The result, completed in 1922, involved five earth dams, 60 miles of levees, channel improvements, 35,000 acres of basin property, 200 floodgates. The task was immense but Dayton has been dry ever since. The $40 million cost, paid for by Miami Valley property owners and public agencies in nine countries, has had direct benefits of well over $90 million. The River Corridor Program has finished the work of making the long-feared river a public amenity. Walkways and bike paths line the Miami in Dayton and other Miami Valley cities.

Johnny Appleseed, Western Reserve, Firelands

The region between Columbus and Cleveland contains some of Ohio's prime farmland and some interesting scenery and people. The territory has never become particularly industrialized, and it's full of charming towns, wineries, orchards, and other agricultural enterprises. Drive slowly through Holmes, Wayne, and Tuscarawas counties. It's Amish country, home of the Plain People, whose religion forbids them to own cars. Highway signs that warn of horse-drawn vehicles will alert you, and the countryside, itself, with its rolling hills and neat farms, will conspire to make you slow down and enjoy the view. It's a good idea. You'll feel better, see more of the scenery, and lessen your chances of an unpleasant meeting with a horse and buggy.

Ashland, seat of Ashland County, was homebase for the legendary Johnny Appleseed. His real name was John Chapman and he owned an orchard over toward Mansfield. Tradition has it that he traveled these parts of Ohio, planting apple orchards wherever he could in the early days of the state. While traveling through this region, Appleseed warned settlers of an imminent Indian attack. The blockhouse where they found safety is preserved in his memory, and you can see a memorial to him in Ashland, one of several that memorialize this itinerant orchardist.

Outside the little town of Lucas is Malabar Farm, a monument to the beginnings of the conservation movement in Ohio in the 1930s. Malabar was the home of Louis Bromfield, a native Ohioan and Pulitzer-prize-winning novelist. Back from a spell overseas in the 1930s, he bought three adjoining farms, depleted and in bad repair. He set out to restore them using all the tools of the conservationist, protecting the woodland, rebuilding the soil, restoring pastures, and writing four books about Malabar. Governors, conservationists, editors, and other public figures were his guests there. Malabar was certainly instrumental in getting the conservation movement the recognition it needed. At Bromfield's death the farm was heavily in debt, but since 1972 Malabar has been the property of the State of Ohio. It's still a working farm and a symbol of the conservation movement that has done so much for Ohio and the nation. It's possible to tour the house and the farm, and a naturalist is there to offer programs of natural history, forest management, and wildlife instruction.

Not far outside of Carey is Indian Trail Caverns, one of Ohio's largest. Like Ohio's other major caverns, this one is caused by percolation of water through underground limestone layers. Unlike the others, this one has natural skylights and a natural stone ladder, features that made it easy for generations of Indians to use the caves for shelter.

The town of Loudonville, replete with rivers, creeks, and a lake within a short drive, considers itself the canoe capital of Ohio. Canoes are for rent at a number of places, and a lot of unspoiled country can be seen from the smooth waterways. Between Loudonville and Wooster are some of the largest remaining inland marshes in the state, especially along Kilbuck Creek. The impoundments of the glaciers, coupled with the area's very slight slope, have been responsible for continual seasonal flooding and permanent wet areas that make excellent nesting ground for waterfowl. The Division of Wildlife manages Kilbuck Creek as a State Wildlife Area, and there's good access via the abandoned B&O railroad grade that parallels the creek. Rabbits, quail, and forest game species can also be seen, occasionally. Dairy farming has been the traditional activity in this part of Ohio, where the land is not too wet for cultivation.

Near Loudonville is the large acreage of Mohican State Park and Forest. Vegetation is inclined toward grand oak-hickory forests where the ground is flat, and some beautiful native pine and hemlock cover the hills. Within the park is the Lyons Falls hiking trail, and a marked nature trail on the north side of Clear Fork is unusually informative. It's a good place for canoeing.

The traveler meandering north and west of Wooster finds himself suddenly approaching the state's most populous areas: Cleveland, Akron, Canton, and Youngstown form a protective ring around the still-rural Western Reserve region in the state's northwest corner.

This book has not chosen cities as a major focus, but it is interesting to think about a portion of this area at a time when the people were at the mercy of the wildlife, rather than the other way around. In 1818, just before Christmas, the men of Medina County organized a hunt in Hinckley Township. Farmers had lost cattle and sheep to marauding wolves and bears, hens were lost to foxes, and deer, raccoons, and squirrels made fast work of cornfields. On December 24, 1818, in the hour just before daylight, 600 settlers took their places on the four sides of Hinckley township, forming a loose battle line that closed as they drew toward the center, making lots of noise and driving the game ahead of them. By good fortune only one hunter was grazed with buckshot, and the only casualties were among the animals: countless squirrels, rabbits, foxes, and 'coons; 17 wolves, 21 bears, and more than 300 deer. One account says the men built a fire and feasted, washing down the hot meat with cold whiskey. A great many Medina County homes had fresh venison for Christmas dinner.

Those days are gone, but the northeastern corner of Ohio has taken care to preserve some strikingly beautiful areas because of their recreational or scenic importance. Portage Lakes State Park, just south of Akron, consists of two lakes created as the summit reservoirs for the Ohio-Erie Canal. The wasting glacier left behind a large outwash belt that, today, consists of gently rolling hills covered with forests of beech and maple.

One of the Akron Metropolitan Parks, below the city of Cuyahoga Falls, has preserved a narrow, constricted gorge through which the river descends 200 feet in about two miles, over many waterfalls and rapids. The gorge was cut when the normal river channel to the south was blocked by glacial fill. The falls for which the city of Cuyahoga Falls was named are now beneath water backed up by the Ohio Edison Company dam.

Farther east at Fredericktown, glaciers had an even greater effect on stream flow: Little Beaver Creek and the North Fork of Little Beaver were blocked by glacial fill and forced to flow the other way by torrential meltwaters. Once north-flowing, they later cut deep gorges for their southward flow to the Ohio. The upland plains are covered with large oaks and white pines, while the cool, moist ravines are home to hemlocks and plants from the pre-glacial period.

Nelson-Kennedy Ledges, a state park between Cleveland and Youngstown is another area that shows the heavily erosive effects of glacial meltwater in the form of scenic ledges and bluffs above the wooded river bottom.

Once through the "urban belt," a bit of New England is visible in the northeastern corner of the state, an area that, interestingly enough, is known as the Western Reserve. The land was reserved for settlement by the State of Connecticut, back when Ohio *was* the west, and the name stuck. In Bath the past is officially preserved at Hale Farm and Western Reserve Village, a re-created town that depicts life from 1800-1850 in this area. Unofficially, it's easy to observe the influence of the early New England settlers in the neat, small towns along the backroads of the less populated counties.

Moving north toward the shore of Lake Erie in Ashtabula County, where a special treat is in store for history buffs. There are 16 covered bridges in the county, tucked away on quiet back roads, mostly used by Amish farmers and an occasional carload of tourists. Spend the day and see them: the one at Harpersfield is one of the longest in the state.

The Lake Erie waterfront has long been valued both for commerce and recreation, and the explorer, today, will find that Lake Erie, today, is a well-developed natural resource. The ports of Ashtabula and Conneaut are among the largest iron-ore receiving centers in the world. Lake freighters unload iron ore here for the mills of Pennsylvania and the Ohio River. But a short distance away, Geneva-on-the-Lake, which offers a variety of commercial amusements as well as camping, has been a popular resort for about 100 years.

Fairport Harbor and adjoining Painesville offer historical exhibits and more of the atmosphere of New England. The lighthouse at Fairport Harbor is one of the oldest in Ohio, and there's a fine view of the lakeshore from the top. Closer to Cleveland is the mile-long beach at Headlands Beach State Park, a popular spot with swimmers from the city on summer weekends.

West of Cleveland is the historic area known as Firelands. Land in this area was granted after the Revolutionary War to compensate people whose home had been burned by the British — hence the name. It's another place where the New England style prevails in older areas. The suburbs of Cleveland stretch westward for about 30 miles along the lake, and around Vermilion the territory once again becomes a resort and recreation-oriented. Sandusky, once known as the world's largest fresh-water fishing center, is also a busy harbor town, and has been playing host to summer guests since the end of the Civil War. There's plenty of access to scenic and recreational areas along the lake, and within miles either side of Sandusky are camping facilities in about a dozen state parks.

From Sandusky it's not far to the Marblehead Peninsula, one of the most picturesque areas in Ohio. The peninsula contains hundreds of acres of orchards and vineyards, juxtaposed against the surf-pounded shores of Lake Erie. Marblehead has been one of the roughest places on the lake since the beginning of navigation in these parts, with occasional northeasters that blow off the lake at hurricane velocity. The Marblehead Lighthouse, erected in 1821 and still in operation, is the oldest on the Great Lakes. The north side of the peninsula is a resort area, and Catawba Peninsula, jutting from the north side of Marblehead, is where you catch the ferryboat for the Lake Erie Islands.

The islands that are scattered throughout Lake Erie have long been popular vacation/resort areas for the people of Ohio. South Bass, with its town of Put-In Bay, is perhaps the best known. Once the site of the luxurious Victory Hotel, a playground for presidents and millionaires, the island has slipped into a pleasant lethargy since the hotel burned in 1919, and there's a state campgound where the Victory once stood. On the east end of the island is a monument to Perry's victory in the Battle of Lake Erie, a significant conflict in the War of 1812. South Bass also has caves, wineries, and fish hatcheries.

Kelleys Island, the largest of the Lake Erie islands, is a scant two miles from shore. An enormous granite slab, Inscription Rock, was carved with graffiti by the Erie Indians who lived there about 350 years ago. One of the most unusual exhibits of the glacial age will be seen here in the Glacial rooves, scorings of glacier-carried stones in the native rock of the island.

Out in Middle Bass, what appears to be a medieval castle is really Lonz's Winery. Visitors are welcome to tour their cool wine cellars.

These are the biggest of the islands, and the most frequently visited of the 20 or so that make up the chain. Others, either privately owned or without dock facilities, are inaccessible to the general public, although boaters may enjoy the waters around them.

Buckeye, Leatherlips

Glaciers didn't make it as far as the Appalachian foothills in the southeastern portion of Ohio, and as a result some of the greatest variety of terrain occurs there. This rough, hilly country, broken everywhere by river gorges, contains most of the forests and a lavish variety of Ohio's native wildlife. Ironically, this is also the area that suffered most in the past from disastrous strip mining, overgrazing, erosion, and flooding. It's the home of the Muskingum Conservancy District, another pioneering effort to maintain the environment.

A lot of history has happened in this area: the Buckeye region received the first settlers who drifted down the Ohio River. The first cross-state canal, from Portsmouth to Cleveland, cut through this country, and remnants of it are preserved. The late 1880s saw drastic disputes in the coal mines of the Hocking Valley: in riots one summer, oil-filled coal cars were set ablaze and pushed into the mineshafts, setting underground fires that burn to this day, occasionally leaking smoke from hillsides and valleys. Ohio's first settlement was in this region — Schoenbrunn, the religious community. Missionaries were forced to clear out during the Revolutionary War, but the buckeye region also claims the oldest permanent settlement: the river town of Marietta has been a going concern since 1788.

Amesville, the first settlement in Athens County was, and is, the site of the famous Coonskin Library. All during the winter of 1804-1805, the men of Amesville ran a trapline, and in the spring they loaded a wagon with bearskins, raccoon skins, wolf hides, and the like, and took them 600 miles to Boston. They traded the skins for $73.50 worth of books, which comprised the entire stock of one of Ohio's earliest lending libraries. The bears, coons, and wolves are gone from Ohio, but the books still exist.

The Ohio River, an influence for every area it touches, is far different here from its languid appearance in the more pastoral regions west of Portsmouth. The river bustles with traffic, and the shoreline is developed to receive the cargoes of dozens of industries. This is coal-mining country, and scores of manufacturing operations are headquartered on the eastern portion of the river. At this point the Ohio is strictly business, though Marietta, in particular, has some interesting museums and historic exhibitions dealing with the river. The lover of nature and scenery will do better to move inland from the river a bit, where orchard, pasture, forest, and lake produce an ambience far different from the purposeful hum of commerce on the river. And once inland, the Muskingum Conservancy District becomes a fact to be dealt with.

In 1938 fourteen flood-control dams were dedicated in a single ceremony, getting the Muskingum Conservancy District off to a fairly auspicious start. The District, which includes about one-fifth of Ohio's area, fans out northward and westward from Marietta as far as Canton, Akron, and Mt. Vernon, a diverse region containing farms, mines, and cities. But, as one commentator pointed out, it all runs downhill. With every flood a great deal of the overworked land washed away to the Gulf of Mexico. Much of the thin, hillside land of this region should never have been cleared or plowed in the first place, and the District is at work to remedy that situation by reforestation and woodland maintenance. Fourteen retaining basins form permanent lakes with several hundred miles of shoreline for recreational use and wildlife management, and many small recreation areas are located at locks and dams along the Muskingum River.

Tappan Lake, 10 miles east of Dennison, is formed by one of the original dams, providing flood and drought control as well as a recreational area. The lake contains the waters of the meandering Stillwater Creek, a tributary of the Tuscarawas River. The dam, 52 feet high and

1,550 feet long, controls drainage of about 70-square miles. The shores are heavily wooded, and blue herons live where the water is shallow.

One of the most spectacular scenic areas in all of Ohio is the Hocking Valley, where the shifting shores of an ancient sea laid down layers of sandstone that have eroded into the deep gorges of Hocking Hills State Park. The once-cultivated hilltops, now returning to forestland through natural succession, do little to prepare you for the deep canyons and impressive waterfalls at the six separate sites within the Hocking State Forest. Perhaps the most spectacular is Ash Cave, a massive sandstone overhang from which a stream drops about 90 feet into a small pool. The cavity behind the falls is a natural amphitheater. The tremendous overhang has remarkable acoustics, and has been used extensively for camp meetings. During April and May the wildflowers are magnificent, and in the winter months the waterfall freezes into a shimmering icy curtain.

Old Man's Cave, west of Logan, is another attraction in the park. Riddled with tunnels and stairways, offering surprising panoramic views, this area was once the home of a hermit for the last years of his life. At the end of the gorge, Old Man's Creek stumbles over a series of ledges and falls 40 feet into a catch pool, and thence over smaller cascades and numerous potholes worn out of the sandstone. The cave, itself, for which this portion of the park is named, is not a cave actually, but a huge overhang, 75 feet above the stream and about 300 feet long. It's another example of soft sandstone sandwiched between harder layers, worn away by running water.

Cedar Falls, Conkle's Hollow, Rock House, and Cantwell Cliffs are the other sites in Hocking Hills State Park. The geological history of the Black Hand sandstone is about the same, but each area offers something a little different. The rugged cliffs, profuse vegetation and shadowy canyons have to be seen to be believed.

A couple of counties away is the Cumberland Mine area, where Ohio Power Company has worked a minor miracle or two in rehabilitating land that had been abused. The Ohio Power Recreation Area in Morgan and Noble Counties is a good example of the ways mankind can put itself on the side of nature and benefit by it. Early settlers cleared the rolling hills of much of the beech and oak forest that once covered them. But typically for his area, the soil was thin and the slopes were steep: farmland wore out and erosion was a problem. The discovery of the rich coal resource underground invited further ecological depredations, and the area was extensively strip-mined until Ohio Power Company began a forestry program to replace the coal with a renewable resource — wood. Thus the land use came in a full circle back to its original woodland state.

Tappan Lake, 10 miles east of Dennison, is formed by one of the original dams, providing flood and drought control as well as a recreational area. The lake contains the waters of the meandering Stillwater Creek, a tributary of the Tuscarawas River. The dam, 52 feet high and 1,550 feet long, controls drainage of about 70-square miles. The shores are heavily wooded, and blue herons live where the water is shallow.

One of the most spectacular scenic areas in all of Ohio is the Hocking Valley, where the shifting shores of an ancient sea laid down layers of sandstone that have eroded into the deep gorges of Hocking Hills State Park. The once-cultivated hilltops, now returning to forestland through natural succession, do little to prepare you for the deep canyons and impressive waterfalls at the six separate sites within the Hocking State Forest. Perhaps the most spectacular is Ash Cave, a massive sandstone overhang from which a stream drops about 90 feet into a small pool. The cavity behind the falls is a natural amphitheater. The tremendous overhang has remarkable acoustics, and has been used extensively for camp meetings. During April and May the wildflowers are magnificent, and in the winter months the waterfall freezes into a shimmering icy curtain.

Old Man's Cave, west of Logan, is another attraction in the park. Riddled with tunnels and stairways, offering surprising panoramic views, this area was once the home of a hermit for the last years of his life. At the end of the gorge, Old Man's Creek stumbles over a series of ledges and falls 40 feet into a catch pool, and thence over smaller cascades and numerous potholes worn out of the sandstone. The cave, itself, for which this

78

portion of the park is named, is not a cave actually, but a huge overhang, 75 feet above the stream and about 300 feet long. It's another example of soft sandstone sandwiched between harder layers, worn away by running water.

Cedar Falls, Conkle's Hollow, Rock House, and Cantwell Cliffs are the other sites in Hocking Hills State Park. The geological history of the Black Hand sandstone is about the same, but each area offers something a little different. The rugged cliffs, profuse vegetation and shadowy canyons have to be seen to be believed.

A couple of counties away is the Cumberland Mine area, where Ohio Power Company has worked a minor miracle or two in rehabilitating land that had been abused. The Ohio Power Recreation Area in Morgan and Noble Counties is a good example of the ways mankind can put itself on the side of nature and benefit by it. Early settlers cleared the rolling hills of much of the beech and oak forest that once covered them. But typically for his area, the soil was thin and the slopes were steep: farmland wore out and erosion was a problem. The discovery of the rich coal resource underground invited further ecological depredations, and the area was extensively strip-mined until Ohio Power Company began a forestry program to replace the coal with a renewable resource — wood. Thus the land use came in a full circle back to its original woodland state.